Life of a Lady Bug

Series- *Children's Nature Quest*

Author

M Borhan

From

Big 6 Publishing

Overview of Ladybug's Life

Ladybugs, small yet vibrant creatures, inhabit gardens and fields, their lifecycle a testament to nature's intricate design. Females lay clusters of eggs near aphid colonies, ensuring food for their voracious larvae. Hatching into spiky larvae, they devour pests relentlessly, transitioning through pupal stages before emerging as iconic, spotted adults.

Their diet consists mainly of aphids and mites, contributing to natural pest control. Ladybugs employ chemical defenses and hibernate in winter, congregating in leaf litter for warmth. Mating in spring, they continue the cycle, their presence a symbol of luck and positivity, cherished by gardeners and farmers worldwide.

Habitat

Ladybugs, also known as ladybirds or lady beetles, typically inhabit gardens, fields, and forests, thriving in areas with an abundance of aphids and other small insects.

Life Cycle

Ladybugs undergo complete metamorphosis, progressing through four stages: egg, larva, pupa, and adult.

They undergo complete metamorphosis, starting as eggs laid near aphid colonies. Hatching into voracious larvae, they consume pests before entering the pupal stage.

Egg-laying

Female ladybugs carefully select sites near aphid colonies, depositing clusters of tiny eggs on leaves or stems.

These eggs hatch into voracious larvae, continuing the cycle of natural pest control.

Eggs

Ladybug eggs hatch into larvae within a few days, before that these eggs are carefully stored by the mother ladybug for the next stage's purposes.

Female ladybugs lay clusters of small, yellow or orange eggs on the undersides of leaves near a food source, such as aphids.

Larval Stage

During the larval stage, ladybugs resemble tiny alligator-like creatures with segmented bodies and spiky appendages. They voraciously consume aphids and other soft-bodied insects, preparing for metamorphosis.

Ladybug larvae are voracious predators, consuming large numbers of aphids and other soft-bodied insects during their 2-4 week larval stage.

Pupa

In the pupa stage, ladybugs undergo a transformative process, immobile and non-feeding, as they prepare to emerge as adults. Encased in a protective casing, they develop into their iconic, spotted form.

So, the larva, after reaching maturity, attaches itself to a leaf or stem and remains into a pupa, a stage where the pupa develops to an adult ladybug.

Young Adult Ladybugs

Emerging from the pupa, the young adult ladybugs are recognizable by the distinctive spotted appearance and small, dome-shaped body.

Diet

Adult ladybugs primarily feed on aphids, mites, and other small insects, making them valuable allies in natural pest control for farmers and gardeners.

Ladybugs also feed on soft-bodied, scale insects, and plant pollen.

Voracious Appetite

The ladybug's most crucial feature is its voracious appetite for aphids, making it an invaluable ally in natural pest control. It is a crucial feature that plays a significant role in agricultural and garden ecosystems by controlling pest populations.

By consuming large numbers of aphids, ladybugs help maintain a balanced ecosystem and reduce the need for chemical pesticides, making them valuable allies to farmers and gardeners in promoting sustainable agriculture practices.

Hibernation*

*Hibernation is a state of reduced metabolic activity and lowered body temperature, typically observed in animals during winter months to conserve energy and survive harsh conditions.

During winter, ladybugs hibernate in clusters, seeking shelter in leaf litter, logs, or other protected locations to survive the colder months.

Chemical Communication
Ladybugs use chemical signals to communicate with each other, aiding in mate attraction and territorial boundaries. 
Ladybugs use pheromones to conduct the chemical behaviors.

Mating*

*Coming together for making eggs

Ladybugs attract mates through chemical signals, and mating often occurs in the spring or early summer.

Fertilization

Female ladybugs can store eggs from multiple mates, using it to fertilize later on, whenever the eggs are needed.

Parental Care

Ladybugs do not provide direct care for their eggs or larvae, but the female chooses egg-laying sites strategically to ensure the survival of her offspring.

Lifespan

Ladybugs generally live for about 1-2 years, with variations depending on the species and environmental conditions.

An Old Mother Ladybug with all its Babies that it had in its Lifespan.

Predation

Birds, spiders, and certain insects prey on ladybugs at various stages of their life cycle.

Defense Mechanism

Ladybugs secrete a yellowish fluid from their leg joints when threatened, emitting a foul odor that deters predators.

Coloration
Ladybugs' bright colors, often red or orange with black spots, serve as a warning to potential predators that they are distasteful or toxic.

Adaptability

Ladybugs can thrive in a variety of environments, adapting to different climates and ecosystems around the world.

Cultural Symbolism

Ladybugs are often considered symbols of good luck and are associated with positive folklore in various cultures worldwide.

Ladybugs, with their vibrant hues and gentle presence, embody nature's affirmation of positivity and harmony, adorning gardens with a symbol of luck and joy.